TOOLS FOR CAREGIVERS

- **F&P LEVEL:** D
- **WORD COUNT:** 58
- **CURRICULUM CONNECTIONS:** directions

Skills to Teach

- **HIGH-FREQUENCY WORDS:** are, in, is, let's, my, that, the, this
- **CONTENT WORDS:** above, ball, behind, below, Ben, bird, box, cat, directions, dog, down, duck's, far, feet, front, hand, learn, left, Mel, near, out, right, up, water, wings
- **PUNCTUATION:** exclamation point, periods
- **WORD STUDY:** long /e/, spelled *ea* (*near*); long /e/, spelled *ee* (*feet*); long /o/, spelled *ow* (*below*); /ow/, spelled *ow* (*down*); /ow/, spelled *ou* (*out*)
- **TEXT TYPE:** factual description

Before Reading Activities

- Read the title and give a simple statement of the main idea.
- Have students "walk" through the book and talk about what they see in the pictures.
- Introduce new vocabulary by having students predict the first letter and locate the word in the text.
- Discuss any unfamiliar concepts that are in the text.

After Reading Activities

Have the readers look around the room. What items are near them? What items are far away? Have readers look out the window. Who or what is outside? Who or what is inside? When readers are in line, who is behind them? Who is in front of them? What other directions and opposites can readers point out around them? Make a list on the board.

Tadpole Books are published by Jump!, 5357 Penn Avenue South, Minneapolis, MN 55419, www.jumplibrary.com

Copyright ©2021 Jump. International copyright reserved in all countries. No part of this book may be reproduced in any form without written permission from the publisher.

Editor: Jenna Gleisner **Designer:** Anna Peterson

Photo Credits: Prostock-studio/Shutterstock, cover (hand); George Panayiotou/Dreamstime, cover (yoyo); imagestock/iStock, 1; VGstockstudio/Shutterstock, 3; Ponomarencko/Dreamstime, 2tl, 2br, 4, 5 (ball); Africa Studio/Shutterstock, 5 (child); Eric Isselee/Shutterstock, 2tr, 2mr, 6–7; Sasin Paraksa/Shutterstock, 8–9 (background); monte_a/Shutterstock, 2ml, 8 (cat); Happy monkey/Shutterstock, 2bl, 9 (dog); bazilfoto/iStock, 10–11; VLADIMIR VK/Shutterstock, 12–13; Wavebreakmedia Ltd/Dreamstime, 14–15; Supachai Panyaviwat/Shutterstock, 16 (pool); juan carlos tinjaca/Shutterstock, 16 (beach ball); nikkytok/Shutterstock, 16 (rubber duck).

Library of Congress Cataloging-in-Publication Data
Names: Kenan, Tessa, author.
Title: Let's learn directions / by Tessa Kenan.
Description: Minneapolis: Jump!, Inc., 2021. | Series: Fun first concepts | Includes index.
Identifiers: LCCN 2020023899 (print) | LCCN 2020023900 (ebook) | ISBN 9781645277651 (hardcover)
ISBN 9781645277668 (paperback) | ISBN 9781645277675 (ebook)
Subjects: LCSH: Orientation—Juvenile literature. | Space perception—Juvenile literature.
English language—Adverb—Juvenile literature.
Classification: LCC BF299.O7 K46175 2021 (print) | LCC BF299.O7 (ebook) | DDC 152.14/2—dc23
LC record available at https://lccn.loc.gov/2020023899
LC ebook record available at https://lccn.loc.gov/2020023900

FUN FIRST CONCEPTS

LET'S LEARN DIRECTIONS

by Tessa Kenan

TABLE OF CONTENTS

Words to Know 2

Directions 3

Let's Review! 16

Index 16

tadpole books

WORDS TO KNOW

down

far

in

near

out

up

DIRECTIONS

Let's learn directions!

ball

The ball is up.

The ball is down.

bird

This bird is near.

That bird is far.

box

The cat is in the box.

The dog is out.

wing

water

The duck's wings are above water.

The duck's feet are below.

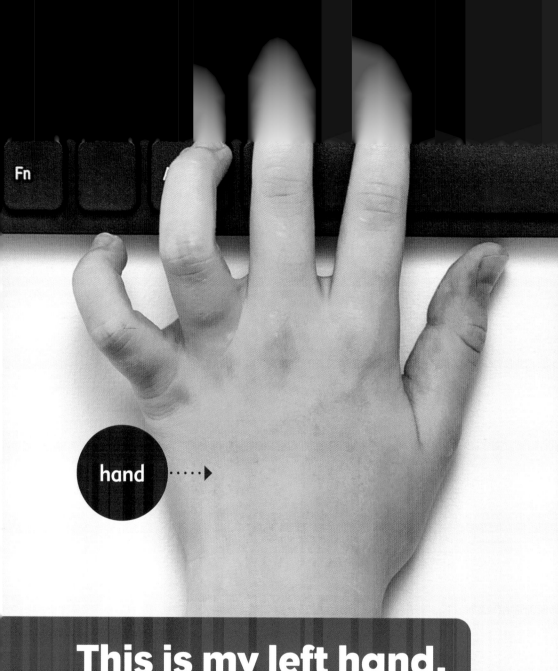

Fn

hand ····▶

This is my left hand.

This is my right hand.

Mel is in front.

Ben is behind.

LET'S REVIEW!

Point to the objects that are in the water. Point to those that are out.

INDEX

ball 4, 5

bird 6, 7

box 8

cat 8

dog 9

duck 10, 11

hand 12, 13

water 10

16